Saving the Earth

One Beard at a Time

(Whether you have one or not)

So, Who Told you you Have to Shave?

So, who told you you have to shave? It was almost half a century ago, but I remember it as clearly as yesterday. Maybe more clearly. Dad said, "There's a razor in the bathroom downstairs, use it." The downstairs bathroom was 'my bathroom', except for when it was Mom's. And except for when anybody else needed to use it. But I slept downstairs and that bathroom was downstairs, so it was 'my bathroom'. I know, I know. TMI (Too much information).

I was thirteen at the time and my beard was coming in just fine.

Yes, there was a razor in that bathroom. Along with a can of shaving cream. But, there were no instructions.

That was before the internet. That was before "How To" or DIY books. That was before shaving commercials. That was before people tried to measure beards with a protractor.

I assumed it would be worse if I asked Dad how I was supposed to shave. In my mind, that would have been pretty much tantamount to blasphemy. I thought I had to figure it out by myself. Sure, I had seen Dad shave, but he had an electric razor. *Mine*, had an honest to goodness razor blade in it. And all

I'd heard about shaving was a comedy skit by Bill Cosby saying, "Zip, Zop, my face was ripped to shreds."

Somehow I figured out how to shave without ripping my face to shreds. I didn't even nick myself. I didn't even need a styptic pencil, which is something you rub on a cut to help it stop bleeding.

Thanks Dad! Thanks a lot Dad!

So, who else told you to shave? One of my first jobs was working at a grocery store. I had slight sideburns in those days. Somehow I set the standard for what the other employees could wear when it came to sideburns (and to bell-bottom jeans). I was also enlisted by classmates in high-school who were trying to change the strict dress code to be less strict. Since my facial growth was accepted by teachers and the principal, they pointed me out and then asked, what's wrong with beards and mustaches? I had neither – only sideburns, but I was still instrumental in their crusade.

In college, I sometimes had a beard. It was variegated – multi-colored – Brown, Black, Red, Grey, and White, even though the variegation doesn't show up well in this picture. My beard is still variegated, but now it's only Black and White. The

once red hairs which are now white, are bristles –
very prickly like cat whiskers.

When I started dating my wife, she said, "You
can keep your beard, but I won't be kissing you."
Needless to say I shaved. But when we're apart for
a while and I'm not working, I let the beard grow
back. When we are together, I still sport sideburns,
leaving plenty of room around my lips to be
kissed. I know, I know, TMI.

So, who told you you have to shave and do you
still have to listen to them?

*My all-time favorite beard is the Bandholz.
Named after its wearer – Eric Bandholz, the
Bandholz beard is about as full as a beard can get.
Eric now sells quality products to care for full
beards.*

What are you Shaving – Face, Legs, Head?

Perhaps you're thinking, I can't even grow a beard, this book doesn't apply to me.

But let me ask you this, are you shaving your legs or head? Perhaps your armpits. Are you a professional swimmer who shaves their entire body?

If you shave and want to save the planet, this book applies to you. If you don't shave then you're already helping save the planet and I hope you'll enjoy reading the rest of this book. If you use personal care products, and most people do, please read the chapter on *Shaving Cream and After Shave* to see what else you can do to save the planet.

If you shave your legs and/or head, could you shave them less or less often? Why not start a fad by shaving patterns on your legs or head? Sorry, somebody already beat you to it. It's called a Mohawk,

Have you considered electrolysis instead of shaving? I'm not considering it, mind you. It sounds painful. But theoretically, I'd only have to do it once and hopefully it's less painful than using tweezers.

Perhaps there's gene therapy to turn off hair growing cells in particular regions.

Are you using the style of razor that works best for you and the earth?

The main issue I have with shaving less often is that when I resume shaving after a couple of days break, the razor pulls my hair. Ouch!

Remembering to use the clipper on my electric razor solves that issue.

Mutton Chops – Mutton Chops are what I normally wear for a beard. Mutton Chops are very thick sideburns. The Mutton Chops beard shown on the Gillette website does not include full sideburns, but is a thick line of sideburns to the chin, extending from there to the sides of the mouth, then up into a mustache. For real Mutton Chop sideburns, think Wolverine, Martin Van Buren, Isaac Asimov, and myself.

Friendly Muttonchops are Muttonchop sideburns connected by a mustache. Not sure how the mustache makes them friendly.

Razor Varieties

These days there are more options with razors. There are Trac-2, Trac-4, Razor Blade razors like my first razor, Straight Razors like those used in Barbershops in old Westerns, and Electric ones. Electric Razors come in battery powered (rechargeable) and plug-in.

I currently use a plug-in electric razor. I had two – one for travel and one for home use. My travel razor had seen its last days and needed replacing. I meant to replace it with another plug-in electric razor. While I'm all for using less electricity to save the plant, my previous experience with rechargables was that the battery would last two years, then you'd have to replace the entire razor and that just made no sense to me.

My wife and I went to the department store. She kept wondering why we weren't heading to the travel section. I finally realized that she wanted to go to the travel section because I was looking for a _travel_ razor. I said, "No, I'm just looking for a razor to take _when_ I travel." We went to the travel section – no razors. Then we went to the personal care section where we found electric razors, but no plug-in ones. They were all rechargables. I guess all the razor companies got on the band wagon to save the earth one beard at a time.

I bought a cheap one. It lasted 2 months, then wouldn't take a charge. I found out I was overcharging it. So I bought a more expensive one, but not the $300 one. I bought one which would tell me when it needed recharging. The first charge lasted a full 4 months – Wow!

We'll see if the batteries last more than two years, but I'm hopeful that they will with all the improvements in rechargeable batteries in the last few years.

During my college years, I discovered that if I used a Trac II razor or similar style, I could skip the shaving cream. (You may want to test this very carefully, before taking it up as a habit.) However, a Trac II razor would only last a month – then it would be so full of nicks I'd have to replace it. Needless to say, I have a very tough beard.

In the long run, it was cheaper, but I felt guilty about throwing so many razors away. So, when I could afford it, I switched to an electric razor. Those blades would eventually wear out, but it took about 7 years. Then I'd replace the razor since that was less expensive than buying new blades. Now, they fairly inexpensive. They're also much more readily available, since you can order them off the internet. Maybe next time, I'll just order new blades.

Electric razors work well for me. They come in two styles – the "Norelco" or three-headed razor style; or the "Braun" or film/shield style. My face has enough nooks and crannies in it that I need the "Norelco" style.

You'll need to decide which style of razor works best for you and for the earth.

I typically wear mutton chops – they're my "trademark", "insignia", "motif" – my signature. That being said, when circumstances permit, I also like to sport a full beard or a Fu Manchu, which is a mustache grown to the chin.

Shaving Cream and After Shave

If you look up the ingredients in Shaving Cream, you may see things like Triethanolomine, Isobutane, Dimethicone, Fragrance, Propane, Iodopropynyl Butylcarbamate, etc. I tend to avoid ingredients I can't pronounce. Those with eth in them come from grain alcohol (ethanol). Isobutane is a form of Butane. Butane is a gas collected when drilling for natural gas or petroleum. Propane is a liquefied petroleum gas. Iodopropynyl Butylcarbamate is a fungicide, meaning it kills fungus. It is toxic enough that its use is limited in some countries.

And then, there's Fragrance. Even natural fragrances in strong doses are harmful. And in most shaving creams the fragrance is not natural. Not natural means, the fragrance is probably derived from petroleum. Many people are sensitive to fragrance, even at low levels. Sensitivity can result in headaches, brain fog, asthma, nerve pain, worry, fear, shortness of breath, and other symptoms. Even if you like fragrance, consider avoiding it for the sake and sanity of others.

I never was fond of aftershave. I tried it once, but it stung like the dickens. Aftershave and cologne have much more fragrance in them than shaving cream. And the fragrance is meant to last all day and longer. That much fragrance can be enough to make somebody dizzy.

If you need/want to use shaving cream and aftershave, try to find natural ones which are fragrance-free. Good luck with the fragrance-free bit on aftershave. There are some brands which say they are fragrance free. But one of the main reasons people use aftershave is for the fragrance.

Some people recommend really cold water, witch hazel (if you like to scream when you slap it on), or jojoba oil instead of aftershave.

I'll just forgo it and save myself the trouble and expense.

Then there's the matter of beard dyes. As you may have noticed, I don't use one. If you want to dye your beard, please use a non-toxic dye or henna. It's better for you, it's better for the planet.

Shaving Less

During my college years, I tried variations on a beard. Just a mustache, a Fu Manchu, Sideburns, a Full Beard. Fu Manchu's looked really nice on me as did Full Beards. Now, when I can't wear a Full Beard, I prefer to wear Full Sideburns.

One way to save the earth is by shaving less – your razor lasts longer, you'll use less shaving cream, you'll use less electricity, etc. And you'll save time and money. Just one person shaving less might not be enough to help, but just imagine if everybody shaved less how much that would shave, I mean save. And now 3-day stubble beards are becoming popular – think Brad Pitt; so why not be fashionable and shave less?

In high school, I'd shave once per day. I would have shaved less often if I could've gotten by with it, but when your beard grows as fast as mine, it's pretty hard to not shave without somebody noticing. In college, I shaved once a day unless I had a date that evening, then I would shave a second time – yes my beard grows that quickly. On some of those days, I dreamed of a time when, like on Star Trek, you wouldn't have to shave due to bio-engineering or whatever the crew used to not have to shave. But I liked my beard, so I didn't dream of that very often.

As I got older, I cared less what people thought and didn't bother to shave twice per day, though sometimes my wife probably wishes I would.

Nowadays, I shave as little as possible and as infrequently as possible, but there are constraints, like love and work. Otherwise I'd wear a full beard all the time.

Just how little can you shave and get by with it?

> *Another favorite beard of mine is the Pharoah beard. One of the nicest Pharaoh beards I've seen was 3 to 4 inches wide, perfectly round, and hung straight down from the chin about 8 inches. No mustache or sideburns on that one.*

More Beard Styles

Gillette lists 15 "popular" styles of beards. These probably work best on the face, but may give you some ideas to try if you're shaving your head or legs instead of your face.

Personally, I don't see people sporting these styles of beards. You can look them up at http://gillette.com/en-us/shaving-tips/facial-hair-styles/beard-styles, if you want pictures. It looks like very precise shaving which may defeat the purpose of shaving to save the earth.

Circle Beard – basically a mustache and beard limited to a circle around the mouth.

Royale Beard – Circle Beard, but there is a space between the ends of the mustache and the beard.

Goatee – doesn't look like what I think of as a Goatee but I guess a Goatee is a beard which solely focuses on the chin, so it qualifies. Gillette also lists a Petite Goatee which again doesn't look like a Goatee to me. Even Uncle Sam wore a Goatee.

A French Fork incorporates a double goatee. Wear one of these and you could be mistaken for a Pirate.

Van Dyke, named after 17th-century Flemish Baroque painter Anthony van Dyck who wore such a beard. So why don't they call it a Van Dyck? Or a Flemish? (Flemish is an ethnic group in Belgium.) A Van Dyke beard is also called a pickedevant. To imagine what a Van Dyke beard looks like, just think of Colonel Sanders.

The Balbo is an extended version of the Van Dyke – Robert Downey Jr sometimes wears one.

Anchor Beard – a mustache, a line from the center of the lower lip down to the chin, plus a beard covering the bottom jaw.

Chevron – supposed to look like a chevron – a line or stripe in the shape of a V or an upside down V. In the case of facial hair, it is a mustache and it is an upside down V. Think Tom Sellick. In the military one chevron usually means a Lance Corporal, a double chevron a Corporal, and triple chevron a Sergeant. When it comes to beards, it's usually a single chevron.

There is also a Painter's Brush mustache which Gillette does not mention. This is a mustache which is a straight line and is thicker than a Pencil

Mustache. A Pencil Mustache is pencil width thick and can be any shape and at any position between the upper lip and the nose.

Gunslinger Beard and Mustache is a thinner version of the Mutton Chops Beard.

Chin Strip is a strip of hair running from lower lip to chin. Chin Strip/Strap Style Beard is a beard running along the lower jaw to the chin. A Chin Curtain is what Lincoln wore – a full beard without mustache or neck hair.

A neck beard only covers the neck and lower jaw.

There seems to be great latitude in what qualifies for what style of beard. I suggest you develop your own style and name it after yourself. Why not start a trend like Bandholz did?

Full Beards include:
- Shenandoah – Bandholz minus the mustache – worn by the Amish
- Garibaldi – more trimmed than the Bandholz
- Dutch – Garibaldi without the mustache
- Razors Edge – full beard and mustache, but not so full sideburns
- Faded Beard – similar to Razors Edge – sideburns are faded on top, but not quite so much as Razors Edge.

The Klingon Beard is a medium length beard. Worf, son of Mogh sported one of these. Before you try and grow one, you might want to check that your intergalactic passport is on order.

Sideburns are also called Side Boards and Side Whiskers, but not by anybody I know. Sideburns are named after General Ambrose Burnside of the Civil War who later became the Governor of Rhode Island. So perhaps they should be called Burnsides or Generals or maybe Ambrosias.

Basically there are two types of Sideburns – Thin and Mutton Chops.

Mustache styles not already mentioned include:
- Walrus – makes you look like a walrus
- Handlebar – ends curl up into a circle (typically achieved by waxing the ends)
- Horseshoe – think Hulk Hogan
- Cowboy – thicker Chevron
- Toothbrush – think Charlie Chaplin.

Wikipedia also includes Clean Shaven as a beard style – really? Isn't that like calling an empty plate a meal?

When thinking about saving the earth by shaving or not shaving, it's sometimes best to keep it simple, whatever style of beard, sideburns, mustache you decide to wear. I tend to keep it simple by shaving less.

I'm surprised more millionaires don't shave. After all, shaving takes time and time is money. Yes, yes, they're millionaires — but just think — if they didn't shave, they might be billionaires. Hey, it could happen.

Cleaning your Razor

Non-electric razors are usually cleaned by running them under water. Electric razors are usually cleaned with a brush designed for that purpose. The newer electric razors can be cleaned by running them under water. I'm still leery of trying that.

If you live in an area which has water shortages, you may want to find a way to clean your razor without water. If you've lost that brush that came with your electric razor, a toothbrush will work just as well, though you probably won't want to use it to brush your teeth with after you've used it to clean your razor.

When I'm at home and clean my electric razor, I brush the hair into a yogurt container. I also collect hair from my comb in that container. When the container is full, I dump it in the compost bin.

Hair is considered a green compost source - https://content.ces.ncsu.edu/backyard-composting-of-yard-garden-and-food-discards. Green compost materials add nitrogen to your compost. Brown materials add carbon to your compost. You want the right ratio of Green to Brown materials in your compost. My rule of thumb is, if it smells or has insects in it, add more brown material – dead leaves if I have them or shredded paper if I don't.

I know that if you grow your hair long and then get it cut, you might be able to donate your hair to Locks of Love or some similar organization to be used in wigs for those who have lost hair due to chemotherapy treatment for cancer.

What about donating beards for those who have lost beards? I don't see anybody doing that, but you might be able to donate you beard hair to Matter of Trust to clean up oil spills.

Excuses for not Shaving

Think about it. You want to save the Earth and you'd prefer not to shave. (If you preferred to shave you probably wouldn't be reading this book.) If nobody shaved or if everybody shaved less, it would help save the earth. It would mean less use of electricity, water, and toxic chemicals.

Beards used to be popular – way back when. Religious people often wore beards, but somewhere along the line many Christians thought it ungodly to be unshaven. Though nobody ever said it in these words, the impression I was given was that I'd never get into heaven with all that facial hair.

These days, many businesses want their employees to be clean shaven, though I've noticed some are relaxing that standard. I think their relaxing it due to the growing popularity of nose rings. And if you're going to let your employees wear facial studs, how can you not allow them to wear facial hair.

But I digress.

My reasons (excuses) for not shaving are:
A) I like the natural look
B) I'm basically lazy

Sometimes those aren't enough for other people and you need a *valid* excuse to not shave. Well, how about Movember – Men's Health Month? Mo is a nickname for Mustache in Australia. Men's Health Month is November. Thus Movember.

During Movember, if your company supports it, men are encouraged to do things that are good for their health and grow facial hair. Women are allowed to participate, though many of them wear fake mustaches rather than growing facial hair. You could be the Movember Ambassador at your company. Some companies have facial hair growing contests.

Another excuse for not shaving – you've gone religious. As mentioned before you may have to go outside of mainstream Christianity for that excuse to be accepted.

You're allergic to shaving.

You're practicing for a bit in a civil war movie or a Western.

You're a bleeder and can't afford to nick your face. You might need a doctor's signature for that one.

You need the extra warmth – this one only works if you live in a cold climate, and then only in winter.

You can't afford it.

Shaving has damaged your skin causing too many painful ingrown hairs. Shaving can lead to infections.

You're covering a scar or a tattoo. I'm covering a mole which is easy enough to nick.

It's too itchy.

It lets people tell you apart from your doppelganger or twin.

You're trying out for a Major League Baseball team.

And, how about this one – your company would like to sell to everybody, but nobody represents the bearded community. So, you're going to do that and reach that community, bringing more sales into the company?

Or how about, I just don't want to and it's none of your business whether I shave or not?

Of course, if I want to be kissed by my wife, I'll continue to forgo facial hair around the lips.

And the number one reason to grow a beard may be, it makes you look like Santa Claus and everybody loves Santa Claus.

OK, well maybe only if your beard is white.

www.ingramcontent.com/pod-product-compliance
Lightning Source LLC
Chambersburg PA
CBHW061955280526

45787CB00004B/1867